Prayers and Practices

for Young Catholics

William H. Sadlier, Inc.
9 Pine Street
New York, New York 10005-1002

MW01048262

CONTENTS

We hold a treasure,
not made of gold,
in earthen vessels,
wealth untold;
one treasure only:
the Lord, the Christ,
in earthen vessels.

Catholic Prayers

Prayer is talking and listening to God. We pray when we thank God for all his gifts, or when we ask him for what we need. We pray when we tell God we are sorry for any wrong we have done, or when we rejoice that God is so good and so full of wonders.

We can pray in many ways and at any time because God is everywhere and always hears us. We can pray using our own words or by just being quiet in his presence. We can pray with the words given us by the Church—prayers that have come down to us over many centuries. Some of these prayers are in the first section of this book.

Sign of the Cross

In the name of the Father,
and of the Son,
and of the Holy Spirit. Amen.

Glory to the Father

Glory to the Father, and to the Son,
and to the Holy Spirit.
As it was in the beginning,
is now, and will be for ever. Amen.

Our Father

Our Father, who art in heaven,
hallowed be thy name;
thy kingdom come;
thy will be done on earth
as it is in heaven.
Give us this day our daily bread;
and forgive us our trespasses
as we forgive those
who trespass against us;
and lead us not into temptation,
but deliver us from evil. Amen.

Matthew

Jude

Bartholomew

Apostles' Creed

I believe in God, the Father almighty,
creator of heaven and earth.

I believe in Jesus Christ,
his only Son, our Lord.
He was conceived by the power
of the Holy Spirit
and born of the Virgin Mary.
He suffered under Pontius Pilate,
was crucified, died, and was buried.
He descended to the dead.
On the third day he rose again.
He ascended into heaven,
and is seated at the right hand
of the Father.
He will come again to judge
the living and the dead.

I believe in the Holy Spirit,
the holy catholic Church,
the communion of saints,
the forgiveness of sins,
the resurrection of the body,
and the life everlasting.
Amen.

Thomas

Simon

Matthias

Prayer of Saint Francis

L ord, make me an instrument of your peace:
where there is hatred, let me sow love;
where there is injury, pardon;
where there is doubt, faith;
where there is despair, hope;
where there is darkness, light;
where there is sadness, joy.

O Divine Master, grant that I may not
so much seek
to be consoled as to console,
to be understood as to understand,
to be loved as to love.

For it is in giving that we receive,
it is in pardoning that we are pardoned,
and it is in dying that we are born
to eternal life.

Prayer of Saint Patrick

Christ be with me, Christ within me,
Christ behind me, Christ before me,
Christ beside me, Christ to win me,
Christ to comfort and restore me,
Christ beneath me, Christ above me,
Christ in quiet, Christ in danger,
Christ in hearts of all that love me,
Christ in mouth of friend or stranger.

Prayer of Saint Richard

Thanks be to you, Lord Jesus Christ,
for all the benefits and blessings
which you have given to me....
O most merciful friend, brother,
and redeemer,
may I know you more clearly,
love you more dearly,
and follow you more nearly.

Morning Prayers

Upon Waking

With your right thumb, trace a small cross on your lips and say:

Lord, open my lips, and my mouth will proclaim your praise.
Liturgy of the Hours

A Morning Offering

My God, I offer you all my prayers, works, and sufferings of this day for all the intentions of your most Sacred Heart. Amen.

Prayer of Blessing

God be in my head,
And in my understanding;

God be in my eyes,
And in my looking;

God be in my mouth,
And in my speaking;

God be in my heart,
And in my thinking;

God be at my end,
And at my departing.
The Sarum Missal

Prayers During the Day

Grace Before Meals

Bless us, O Lord, and these
   your gifts which we are about
to receive from your bounty,
through Christ our Lord. Amen.

Grace After Meals

We give you thanks, almighty God,
   for these benefits and all
your gifts which we have received,
through Christ our Lord. Amen.

Act of Faith

O God, we believe in all that Jesus has
   taught us about you. We place all our
trust in you because of your great love
for us.

Act of Hope

O God, we never give up on your love.
   We have hope and will work for your
kingdom to come and for a life that lasts
forever with you in heaven.

Act of Love

O God, we love you above all things.
   Help us to love ourselves and one
another as Jesus taught us to do.

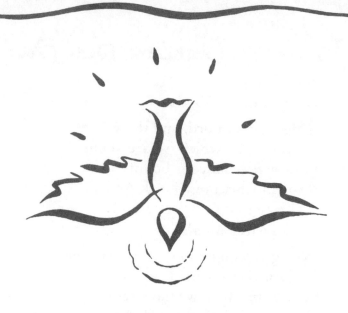

Prayer to the Holy Spirit

V. Come, Holy Spirit, fill the hearts of your faithful.
R. And kindle in them the fire of your love.

V. Send forth your Spirit and they shall be created.
R. And you will renew the face of the earth.

Let us pray.

Lord,
by the light of the Holy Spirit
you have taught the hearts of your faithful.
In the same Spirit
help us to relish what is right
and always rejoice in your consolation.

We ask this through Christ our Lord.
R. Amen.

Prayers from the Psalms

Psalm of Praise

O LORD, our Lord,
how awesome is your name
through all the earth!

Psalm 8:2

Psalm of Contrition

You are my shelter; from distress you
keep me;
with safety you ring me round.

Psalm 32:7

Psalm of Thanksgiving

I thank you, LORD, with all my heart.
I praise your name for your fidelity
and love.

Psalm 138:1, 2

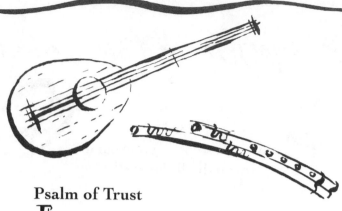

Psalm of Trust

For in God our hearts rejoice;
    and in your holy name we trust.
May your kindness, LORD, be upon us;
    we have put our hope in you.

Psalm 33:21–22

Psalm for Help

Remember me, LORD, as you favor
    your people;
come to me with your saving help.

Psalm 106:4

Psalm of Petition

Hear my voice, LORD, when I call;
    have mercy on me and answer me.
LORD, show me your way;
    lead me on a level path.

Psalm 27:7, 11

Psalm of Quiet Confidence

But I trust in you, LORD;
    I say, "You are my God."
My times are in your hands.

Psalm 31:15–16

Evening Prayers

Act of Contrition

My God,
I am sorry for my sins with all my heart.
In choosing to do wrong
and failing to do good,
I have sinned against you,
whom I should love above all things.
I firmly intend, with your help,
to do penance,
to sin no more,
and to avoid whatever leads me to sin.
Our Savior Jesus Christ
suffered and died for us.
In his name, my God, have mercy.

Rite of Penance

Saint Teresa's Bookmark

Let nothing disturb you.
Let nothing frighten you.
All things are passing
but God never changes.
Patience gains all things.
If you have God, you
need nothing else.

Saint Teresa of Avila

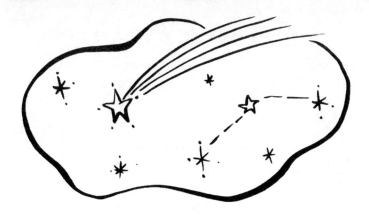

Prayer for My Vocation

Dear God,
You have a great and loving plan
for our world and for me.
I wish to share in that plan fully,
faithfully, and joyfully.
Help me to understand what it is
you wish me to do with my life.
Help me to be attentive to the signs
that you give me about preparing
for the future.
And once I have heard and understood
your call, give me the strength
and the grace to follow it
with generosity and love.

Night Prayer

Dear God, before I sleep
I want to thank you for this day
so full of your kindness and your joy.
I close my eyes to rest,
safe in your loving care.

Prayers for the Dead

These prayers are familiar to many Catholics. They are part of the funeral liturgy and are often prayed at other times, too. You might want to learn these prayers by heart.

Eternal rest grant unto them, O Lord, and let perpetual light shine upon them. May they rest in peace. Amen. May their souls, and the souls of all the faithful departed, through the mercy of God, rest in peace. Amen.

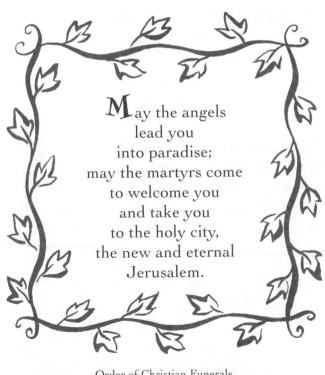

May the angels
lead you
into paradise;
may the martyrs come
to welcome you
and take you
to the holy city,
the new and eternal
Jerusalem.

Order of Christian Funerals

Prayers to Mary

Hail Mary

Hail Mary, full of grace,
the Lord is with you;
blessed are you among women,
and blessed is the fruit
of your womb, Jesus.
Holy Mary, Mother of God,
pray for us sinners now
and at the hour of our death. Amen.

Hail, Holy Queen

Hail, Holy Queen, Mother of Mercy,
our life, our sweetness,
and our hope! To you do we cry,
poor banished children of Eve;
to you do we send up our sighs,
mourning and weeping in this valley of tears.

Turn, then, most gracious advocate,
your eyes of mercy toward us;
and after this our exile, show unto us
the blessed fruit of your womb, Jesus,
O clement, O loving, O sweet Virgin Mary!

The Angelus

T he angel of the Lord declared to Mary,
and she conceived by the Holy Spirit.
Hail Mary....

Behold the handmaid of the Lord,
be it done to me according to your word.
Hail Mary....

And the Word was made flesh
and dwelled among us.
Hail Mary....

Pray for us, O Holy Mother of God,
that we may be made worthy of
the promises of Christ.

Let us pray:

Pour forth, we beseech you, O Lord, your
grace into our hearts, that we to whom the
incarnation of Christ your Son was made
known by the message of an angel may, by his
passion and death, be brought to the glory of
his resurrection, through Christ our Lord.
Amen.

The Litany of the Blessed Virgin Mary

In this litany we pray by using some of the titles of the Blessed Virgin Mary. These titles help us to remember Mary's role in God's plan of salvation. What follows is part of the litany.

The response to each special title is "Pray for us."

Holy Mary,
Holy Mother of God,
Holy Virgin of virgins,
Mother of Christ,
Mother most pure,
Mother most lovable,
Mother of our Creator,
Mother of our Savior,
Virgin most faithful,
Cause of our joy,
Health of the sick,
Refuge of sinners,
Comfort of the afflicted,
Help of Christians,
Queen of angels,
Queen of apostles,
Queen of martyrs,
Queen of all saints,
Queen conceived without original sin,
Queen of the most holy rosary,
Queen of families,
Queen of peace,

Leader: Pray for us, O Holy Mother of God.

All: That we may be made worthy of the promises of Christ.

The Memorare

Remember, O most gracious Virgin Mary, that never was it known that anyone who fled to your protection, implored your help, or sought your intercession was left unaided. Inspired with this confidence, we fly unto you, O Virgin of virgins, our Mother. To you we come, before you we kneel, sinful and sorrowful. O Mother of the Word made flesh, do not despise our petitions, but in your mercy hear and answer them. Amen.

Praying with God's Word

One day Jesus got into a boat with his disciples. As they were sailing, Jesus fell asleep. According to Luke:

A squall blew over the lake, and they were taking in water and were in danger. They came and woke him saying, "Master, master, we are perishing!" He awakened, rebuked the wind and the waves, and they subsided and there was a calm.
Luke 8:23–24

Pray in these words or your own:

Jesus, when a storm comes up in my life, calm my fears.

When I am afraid to do what I know is right, give me courage.

When I am afraid to try something new because I might fail, give me hope.

When I have a problem that is too big to handle alone, give me trust in you and in those who can help me.

Dear God,
be good to me.
The sea is
so wide, and
my boat
is so small.

Fishers of
Brittany, France

Quiet Prayer

Prayer of Inner Stillness

Choose a time when you can be alone. Sit in a comfortable position and relax by breathing deeply. Try to shut out all the sights and sounds around you so that you feel the peaceful rhythm of your breathing in and out.

Slowly repeat a short prayer such as "**Come, Lord Jesus**" *or perhaps just the name* "*Jesus.*"

A Scripture Meditation

✣ Pray for inner stillness.

✣ Read something in the Bible about Jesus.

✣ Close your eyes and imagine you are with Jesus.

✣ Talk to Jesus about what the reading means to you.

Catholic Life and Practices

The Church is almost two thousand years old. During that long time, the followers of Jesus Christ have tried in many ways to remember, to do, and to teach what Jesus taught. They have tried to live as Jesus lived. They want to pass on to their children, and to future generations, this way of life with its important teachings and practices. Some of these practices, which help make faith deeper and more real in our lives, are described in this book. All of them have been approved by the Church and are given to us today to help us to become better followers of Jesus. They are all a precious part of our inheritance as Catholics.

The Eucharist

On the night before he died for us, Jesus shared the Last Supper with his apostles. Taking bread, he blessed it and broke it. Then he gave it to them, saying, "This is my body, which will be given for you; do this in memory of me." Then he gave them a cup, saying, "This cup is the new covenant in my blood, which will be shed for you" (Luke 22:19, 20).

Ever since that Last Supper, the Church has continued to do what Jesus told us to do. By the power of the Holy Spirit and through the words and actions of the priest, our gifts of bread and wine become the Body and Blood of Christ. This is the sacrament of the Eucharist. Jesus is really present in the Eucharist.

The word **Eucharist** means "to give thanks." Our celebration of the Eucharist is called the Mass. At Mass we remember all that Jesus did to save us, and we give thanks to God our Father. We share in Jesus' sacrifice on the cross. That is why the Mass is a sacrifice. The Mass is also a meal because we receive Jesus, the Bread of Life, in Holy Communion.

To show respect and love for Jesus, Catholics fast before receiving Holy Communion. This means that we do not eat or drink anything —except water and medicine—for one hour before Communion.

Communion Prayers

Lord, I am not worthy to receive you, but
  only say the word and I shall be healed.

The Sacramentary

Prayer Before Communion

Jesus,
you are God-with-us,
especially in this sacrament
of the Eucharist.
You love me as I am
and help me grow.

Come and be with me
in all my joys and sorrows.
Help me share your peace and love
with everyone I meet.

Prayer After Communion

Jesus, Son of God,
  thanks and praise to you.

Jesus, Good Shepherd,
  thanks and praise to you.

Jesus, Lamb of God,
  thanks and praise to you.

Jesus, Bread of life and love,
  thanks and praise to you.

Jesus, Source of strength and joy,
  thanks and praise to you.

Thank you, Jesus, for your life
in mine. Help me live your good
news of love and peace.

Visits to the Blessed Sacrament

After we receive the Body and Blood of Christ at Mass, the Hosts that remain are placed in the tabernacle. A special light, called the sanctuary lamp, is always kept burning nearby. This light reminds us that Jesus Christ is present in the Blessed Sacrament. We show reverence for Jesus, who is really present in the Eucharist. We do this by genuflecting, or bending the right knee to the floor, in front of the tabernacle.

We often go into church at times other than the celebration of Mass and the sacraments to "make a visit"—to take a few minutes to tell Jesus of our love, our needs, our hopes, and our thanks.

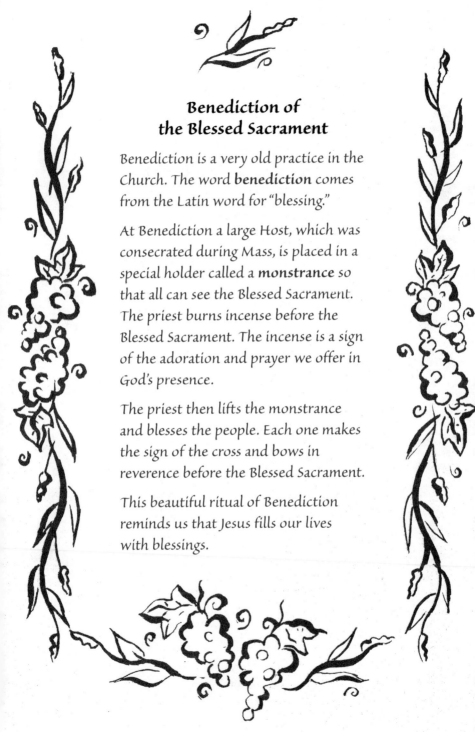

Benediction of the Blessed Sacrament

Benediction is a very old practice in the Church. The word **benediction** comes from the Latin word for "blessing."

At Benediction a large Host, which was consecrated during Mass, is placed in a special holder called a **monstrance** so that all can see the Blessed Sacrament. The priest burns incense before the Blessed Sacrament. The incense is a sign of the adoration and prayer we offer in God's presence.

The priest then lifts the monstrance and blesses the people. Each one makes the sign of the cross and bows in reverence before the Blessed Sacrament.

This beautiful ritual of Benediction reminds us that Jesus fills our lives with blessings.

The Sacrament of Reconciliation

Jesus Christ, the only Son of God, showed us how to live and how to love. Jesus taught us that to be truly God's children we must live according to the Ten Commandments (see page 35) and the Law of Love. The Law of Love is this:

✣ We must love God with all our hearts.

✣ We must love our neighbor as we love ourselves.

Sometimes we fail to live as God wants us to live. When we do something that we know is against God's law, we sin. God never stops loving us, even when we sin. To bring us back to forgiveness and love, God has given us the sacrament of Reconciliation. This is how to receive Reconciliation:

✣ I examine my conscience.

✣ I confess my sins to the priest.

✣ The priest gives me a penance.

✣ I say an act of contrition (see page 15).

✣ The priest gives me absolution.

An Examination of Conscience

I examine my conscience by thinking about my thoughts and actions. I ask myself whether I have loved God, others, and myself. (Remember: temptations, accidents, and mistakes are not sins.) Here are some questions to ask.

Love God with all your heart.

✣ Does God come first in my life, or are other things more important to me?

✣ Do I go to Mass and participate each week?

✣ Do I use God's name carelessly or in anger?

Love others.

✣ Do I obey my parents and those who are responsible for me?

✣ Am I honest and truthful or have I taken something that belongs to others? Have I cheated? Have I lied?

✣ Have I said unkind things about others?

✣ Have I tried to be kind to others?

Love yourself.

✣ Do I respect and take care of my body?

✣ Do I eat properly?

✣ Do I avoid harmful things like drugs, tobacco, and alcohol?

The Law of Love

Once, while Jesus was teaching, someone asked him which commandment was the greatest. Jesus replied:

> "You shall love the Lord, your God, with all your heart, with all your soul, and with all your mind. This is the greatest and the first commandment. The second is like it: You shall love your neighbor as yourself."
>
> Matthew 22: 37–39

When we live the Law of Love, we know we are doing what God wants us to do. This is how we follow Jesus each day of our lives.

The Ten Commandments

The first three commandments help us to love and honor God.

The last seven commandments help us to love others and ourselves.

1. I am the Lord your God, who brought you out of slavery. Worship no god except me.

2. You shall not misuse the name of the Lord your God.

3. Remember to keep holy the Sabbath day.

4. Honor your father and your mother.

5. You shall not kill.

6. You shall not commit adultery.

7. You shall not steal.

8. You shall not tell lies against your neighbor.

9. You shall not want to take your neighbor's wife or husband.

10. You shall not want to take your neighbor's possessions.

Based on Exodus 20:1–17

The Beatitudes

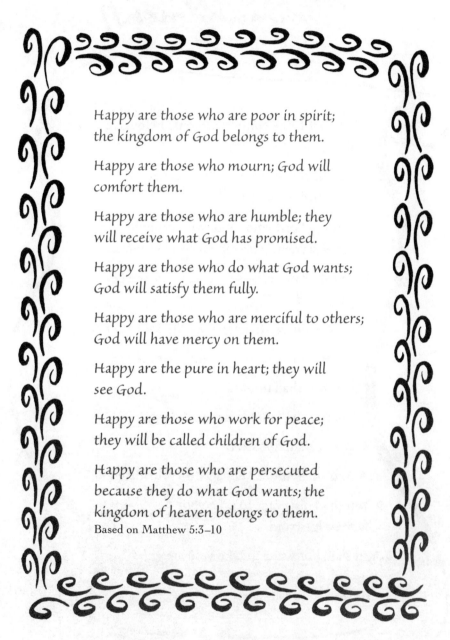

Happy are those who are poor in spirit;
the kingdom of God belongs to them.

Happy are those who mourn; God will
comfort them.

Happy are those who are humble; they
will receive what God has promised.

Happy are those who do what God wants;
God will satisfy them fully.

Happy are those who are merciful to others;
God will have mercy on them.

Happy are the pure in heart; they will
see God.

Happy are those who work for peace;
they will be called children of God.

Happy are those who are persecuted
because they do what God wants; the
kingdom of heaven belongs to them.
Based on Matthew 5:3–10

The Works of Mercy

The Corporal Works of Mercy

✤ Feed the hungry.
✤ Give drink to the thirsty.
✤ Clothe the naked.
✤ Help those imprisoned.
✤ Shelter the homeless.
✤ Care for the sick.
✤ Bury the dead.

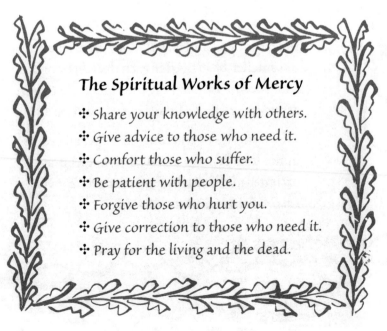

The Spiritual Works of Mercy

✤ Share your knowledge with others.
✤ Give advice to those who need it.
✤ Comfort those who suffer.
✤ Be patient with people.
✤ Forgive those who hurt you.
✤ Give correction to those who need it.
✤ Pray for the living and the dead.

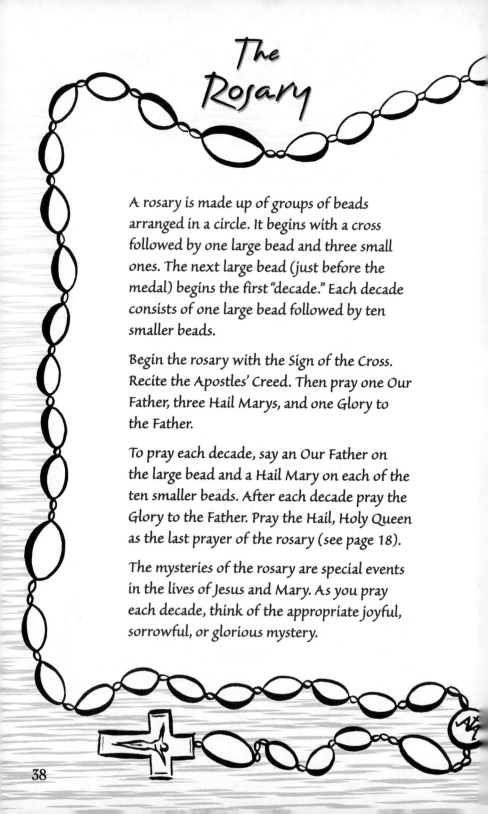

The Rosary

A rosary is made up of groups of beads arranged in a circle. It begins with a cross followed by one large bead and three small ones. The next large bead (just before the medal) begins the first "decade." Each decade consists of one large bead followed by ten smaller beads.

Begin the rosary with the Sign of the Cross. Recite the Apostles' Creed. Then pray one Our Father, three Hail Marys, and one Glory to the Father.

To pray each decade, say an Our Father on the large bead and a Hail Mary on each of the ten smaller beads. After each decade pray the Glory to the Father. Pray the Hail, Holy Queen as the last prayer of the rosary (see page 18).

The mysteries of the rosary are special events in the lives of Jesus and Mary. As you pray each decade, think of the appropriate joyful, sorrowful, or glorious mystery.

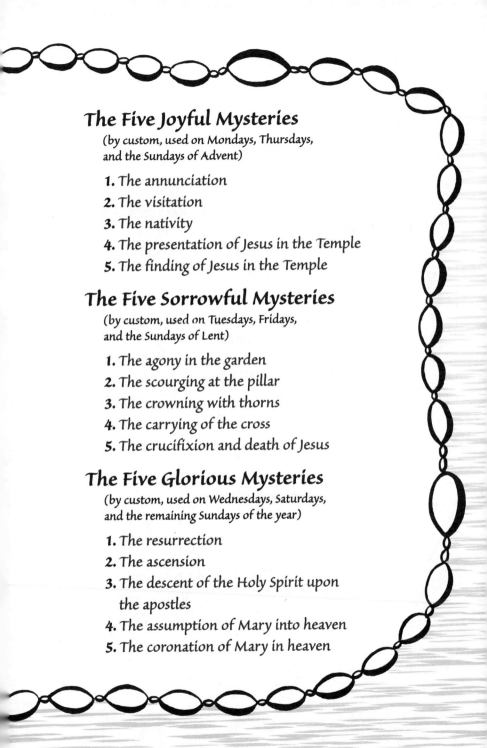

The Five Joyful Mysteries

*(by custom, used on Mondays, Thursdays,
and the Sundays of Advent)*

1. The annunciation

2. The visitation

3. The nativity

4. The presentation of Jesus in the Temple

5. The finding of Jesus in the Temple

The Five Sorrowful Mysteries

*(by custom, used on Tuesdays, Fridays,
and the Sundays of Lent)*

1. The agony in the garden

2. The scourging at the pillar

3. The crowning with thorns

4. The carrying of the cross

5. The crucifixion and death of Jesus

The Five Glorious Mysteries

*(by custom, used on Wednesdays, Saturdays,
and the remaining Sundays of the year)*

1. The resurrection

2. The ascension

3. The descent of the Holy Spirit upon
the apostles

4. The assumption of Mary into heaven

5. The coronation of Mary in heaven

The Liturgical Year

Ordinary

Christmas

Advent

Spring, summer, winter, and fall make up the four seasons of our natural year. The Church year also has seasons of prayer that remind us of Jesus' life, death, and resurrection. The liturgical year, with its special seasons, helps us to remember that all time is holy, and that every season is a season to be lived in the presence of God.

The Advent Season

The liturgical year begins with Advent, the four weeks of preparation for Christmas.

The Christmas Season

During the Christmas season, we celebrate the birth of Jesus and the announcement to the whole world that he is the promised Messiah and the Savior of all.

The Lenten Season

During the season of Lent, we prepare for Easter and for the renewal of our baptismal promises. Lent begins

Ordinary

Time

Lent

Easter Triduum

Easter

on Ash Wednesday and
continues until Holy Thursday.

The Easter Triduum

The word triduum means "three days." The Easter
Triduum is a period of three days from Holy
Thursday evening until Easter Sunday evening.
This is the most important time of the Church year.

The Easter Season

The greatest feast of the liturgical year is Easter
Sunday, the day we celebrate Jesus' resurrection and
our new life with God. The Easter season continues
for fifty days until Pentecost Sunday.

Ordinary Time

Ordinary Time includes the weeks of the year
that are not part of the seasons of Advent,
Christmas, Lent, the Triduum, or
Easter. The Church reminds us that,
no matter what the season, God
is always with us, present and
active in our lives.

Time

Prayers for Church Seasons

Advent

The Blessing of an Advent Wreath

Leader:

> Lord God,
> let your blessing come upon us
> as we light the candles of this
> wreath.
> May the wreath and its light
> be a sign of Christ's promise to bring
> us salvation.
> May he come quickly and not delay.
> We ask this through Christ our Lord.

All: **Amen.**

Catholic Household Blessings and Prayers

(The leader then prays the petition for the week. All respond: "Come, Lord Jesus! Alleluia!" Then the candle for that week is lit.)

First Candle:

> Come, Lord Jesus! Bring us mercy.

Second Candle:

> Come, Lord Jesus! Bring us hope.

Third Candle:

> Come, Lord Jesus! Bring us joy.

Fourth Candle:

> Come, Lord Jesus! Bring us peace.

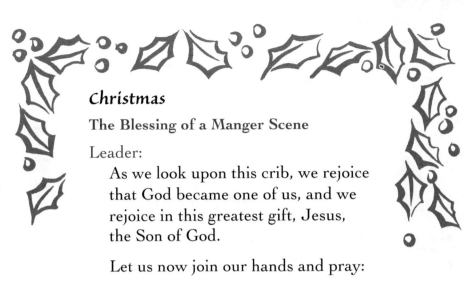

Christmas

The Blessing of a Manger Scene

Leader:

As we look upon this crib, we rejoice
that God became one of us, and we
rejoice in this greatest gift, Jesus,
the Son of God.

Let us now join our hands and pray:

God of every nation and people,
from the very beginning of creation
you have made manifest your love;
when our need for a Savior was great
you sent your Son to be born of the
    Virgin Mary.
To our lives he brings joy and peace,
justice, mercy, and love.

Lord,
bless all who look upon this manger;
may it remind us of the humble birth
    of Jesus,
and raise up our thoughts to him,
who is God-with-us and Savior of all,
and who lives and reigns for ever
    and ever.

All: Amen.

Catholic Household Blessings and Prayers

Lent

From the earliest days of the Church, Christians remembered Jesus' life and death by visiting and praying at the places where Jesus lived, suffered, died, and rose from the dead.

As the Church spread to other countries, not everyone could travel to the Holy Land. So local churches began inviting people to "follow in the footsteps of Jesus" without leaving home. "Stations," or places to stop and pray, were made so that stay-at-home pilgrims could "walk the way of the cross" in their own parish churches. We do the same today, especially during Lent.

The Stations of the Cross

1. Jesus is condemned to die.
2. Jesus takes up his cross.
3. Jesus falls the first time.
4. Jesus meets his mother.
5. Simon helps Jesus carry his cross.
6. Veronica wipes the face of Jesus.
7. Jesus falls the second time.
8. Jesus meets the women of Jerusalem.
9. Jesus falls the third time.
10. Jesus is stripped of his garments.
11. Jesus is nailed to the cross.
12. Jesus dies on the cross.
13. Jesus is taken down from the cross.
14. Jesus is laid in the tomb.

Ash Wednesday

Ash Wednesday is the first day of Lent. On this day, the palms blessed the year before on Palm Sunday are burned. Then the ashes are blessed by the priest.

As our foreheads are marked with the sign of the cross, the priest or minister says,

> "Turn away from sin and be faithful
> to the gospel," or,
> "Remember, you are dust
> and to dust you will return."

Ashes are an ancient sign of sorrow for sin and repentance.

Holy Week

Holy Week begins with Palm (Passion) Sunday, when we celebrate the entrance of Jesus into Jerusalem. We honor Jesus by carrying palm branches and singing:

> "Hosanna to the Son of David,
> the King of Israel.
> Blessed is he who comes
> in the name of the Lord.
> Hosanna in the highest."
> **Rites for Holy Week**

On this day, palms are blessed and given out to the people, who hold them during the reading of the gospel. Many Christians bring palms home and keep them as a remembrance of the saving work of Jesus Christ, our Savior and King.

The Easter Triduum

Holy Thursday

In the evening, we gather for the Mass of the Lord's Supper. At this Mass, we remember the Last Supper in a special way, when Jesus gave us the gift of His Body and Blood. We also recall that Jesus washed the feet of his disciples as a symbol of service. Today the pope, the bishops, and our own parish priests imitate Jesus in this beautiful way.

Good Friday

On this day the Church remembers the Lord's passion and death. At an afternoon liturgy, we listen to the Scriptures, we give special honor to the cross, and we receive Holy Communion. (Mass itself is not celebrated.) For the whole Church, Good Friday is a solemn day of prayer.

Holy Saturday

On this day the whole Church quietly remembers the sacrifice of Jesus. It is as if we are all waiting at the tomb, preparing to greet the risen Lord. At night we will begin our celebration of Jesus' resurrection at the Easter Vigil.

At the Easter Vigil, the large paschal candle is blessed and lit to remind us that Jesus is the Light of the World. We pray this prayer:

M ay the light of Christ,
      rising in glory,
      dispel the darkness of our
         hearts and minds.

The Sacramentary

During the Easter Vigil, we welcome new members into the Church. We also renew our own baptismal promises. We then join in celebrating a joyful Easter Eucharist!

Easter Sunday

On Easter Sunday we pray:

M ay the risen Lord
      breathe on our minds and
         open our eyes
that we may know him in the
      breaking of bread,
and follow him in his risen life.
Grant this through Christ our Lord.
Amen.

The Sacramentary

On Pentecost, we remember the day the Holy Spirit came to Jesus' first disciples. The Holy Spirit helps us to live as God's people.

Thank you, risen Christ, for the gift of the Holy Spirit!

Ordinary Time

A Blessing for Our Family

Leader:

As we gather as a family to ask God's blessing, we remember Jesus, Mary, and Joseph. They loved one another and shared their joys and sorrows together. With the Holy Family, all the angels and saints, and the members of our family who are with God, let us pray:

God, bless our family, both near and far. Protect us from all harm and need. May your blessing bring peace and strength, and may our love for one another extend beyond these walls to all the world. We ask this through Christ our Lord.

All: Amen.

(Family members may exchange a hug or another sign of peace.)